big difference.
Maxx
Velde '98

is for Extant

Written and Illustrated by Maxx Velde

For the animals
we didn't save.

Information from:

iucnredlist.org

nationalgeographic.com

rainforests.mongabay.com

worldwildlife.org

defenders.org

mnn.com

earthsendangered.com

wildlife.ca.gov

thespruce.com

wildlifecenter.org

seethewild.org

onegreenplanet.org

a-z-animals.com

orangutan.org

whales.org

whalemuseum.org

numbat.org.au

savetherhino.org

wildmadagascar.org

onekindplanet.org

What do these mean?

 **is for** Habitat Loss
The animal is threatened because their habitat is shrinking, usually due to human developement.

 **is for** Pollution
The animal is threatened because of human waste, often through plastic and chemicals.

 **is for** Climate Change
The animal is threatened because of increasing global temperatures.

 **is for** Hunting
The animal is threatened because they or something in their food web is being over-hunted.

 **is for** Invasive Species
The animal is threatened because a non-native species was introduced to their habit and is disrupting the area's food web.

A is for Anteater
(Pictured: Giant Anteater)

Region: Forested and grassland areas in Central and South America

Status: Vulnerable

Facts:
Anteaters prefer to live by themselves, so they don't have to worry about sharing food. Anteaters use their two-foot long tongue to eat around 30,000 ants and termites every day! They're careful to keep the colonies in tact, so they can return later for more food.

How we can help:
Be aware of how much paper you use. Paper is made from trees, and chopping down trees in South America gives anteaters less space to live.

B is for Bee

Region: Worldwide

Status: Endangered

Facts:

Bees are pollinators, meaning they transfer pollen from plant to plant, allowing more to grow. They buzz to shake pollen off of flowers and carry the pollen on their legs. Roughly 1/3 of what humans eat is pollinated by bees. Without bees, we would lose a lot of food!

How we can help:

Plant bee-friendly gardens using native plants. Build "Bee Condos" by drilling holes into a thick block of wood.

C is for Coral

Region: Worldwide
Status: Vanishing

Facts:
Even though they don't look like it, coral are animals too! The hard, colorful part of coral acts as an exoskeleton for the small animals, called polyps inside. Coral reefs act as a shelter, source of food, and birthplace for many marine organisms. Many parts of coral reefs can be used in medicine for humans.

How we can help:
Reduce, re-use, recycle! Conserve water. More pollution in the water can change its chemistry, making it dangerous to living things.

D is for Dolphin

Region: Worldwide

Status: Vulnerable—Critically Endangered

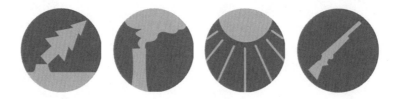

Facts:

Dolphins have been observed to be very social and playful animals, and are believed to be among the smartest animals on the planet. They communicate using echolocation, making loud clicks and whistling noises to communicate over long distances.

How we can help:

Recycle and save water. Use Seafood Watch and eat sustainable seafood. Dolphins can get caught in nets if fishing boats aren't careful.

E is for Elephant

Region: Savanna and forested areas in Africa and Southern Asia

Status: Vulnerable—Critically Endangered

Facts:
Elephants are very smart and have a great memory. This helps them find watering holes during dry seasons. Female elephants tend to travel together, while male elephants usually leave the group between ages 12 and 15.

How we can help:
Stay away from ivory! It's made from an elephant's tusks. Buy products that are FSC (Forest Stewardship Council) certified.

F is for Frog

(Pictured, from top left to bottom right:
Lemur Leaf, Dyeing Dart, Black-Eyed Leaf,
Honduran Brook, William's Bright-Eyed)
Region: Worldwide, damp areas
Status: Vulnerable—Critically Endangered

Facts:

Frogs are amphibians, meaning they begin their
lives breathing water, but breathe air when they get
older. Frogs begin their lives as tadpoles and over
time lose their tail and grow legs. Some frogs will
lay their eggs in small pools of water collected in
plants, or even carry them on their back.

How we can help:

Save water and don't litter! Frogs can absorb liquids
through their skin and that includes any chemicals
that have mixed with the water.

G is for Gorilla

Region: Tropical areas in Africa
Status: Critically Endangered

Facts:
Despite their size and strength, gorillas are mostly herbivores. They only eat plants and bugs! Gorillas are very social, travelling in groups of at least 5-10. They're also very intelligent, and some have even been taught to speak sign language by humans.

How we can help:
Buy products that are FSC-certified. It's the best way to make sure trees aren't being taken away from the gorillas' habitat.

H is for Hammerhead Shark

Region: Worldwide, oceans and coastlines

Status: Vulnerable—Endangered

Facts:
Hammerhead sharks have a sensor in their strangely-shaped heads that allow them to detect electrical fields, and essentially find prey by "feeling" its movements. Hammerhead sharks are not considered to be dangerous to people, though it's smart to keep a safe distance from them.

How we can help:
Eat less seafood and if you do, eat sustainable seafood. Sharks are often tangled in the nets of unsafe fishing boats.

I is for Iguana
(Pictured: Marine Iguana)

Region: Galápagos Islands

Status: Vulnerable

Facts:

Marine Iguanas are the only species of marine lizard. They spend a lot of time warming up their bodies by basking on seaside rocks, before diving into the cold waters to dine on green algae. The salt from the seawater is bad for the iguanas, so they sneeze the extra salt out of their noses!

How we can help:

Don't pollute, and use less water when possible.

J is for Japanese Macaque

Region: Tropical forests and
Mountains in Japan

Status: Vulnerable

Facts:

Japanese Macaques are very social monkeys
and tend to live in large groups. They can
survive in very cold temperatures, as low as
-5 degrees farenheit, but they like to keep
warm by bathing in hot springs. Besides
humans, they are the only animal known to
clean their food before eating it.

How we can help:

Expressing your interest in wildlife can
encourage governments to put more effort
into conservation.

K is for Killer Whale

Region: Worldwide

Status: Endangered and Vulnerable in some areas

Facts:
Killer whales (also known as orcas) are actually the world's largest species of dolphins despite most people calling them whales.
They travel in groups, called pods, of up to 40 individuals. Like other species of dolphins, they communicate with echolocation.

How we can help:
Eat sustainable seafood. Keep the oceans clean by not polluting.

L is for Leaf-Tailed Gecko

Region: Madagascar

Status: Vulnerable

Facts:
Leaf-tailed geckos use their excellent camouflage to hide from predators. With their green and brown colors and leaf-shaped tail, they blend seamlessly among the trees. Geckos have sticky pads on their feet that make climbing up vertical surfaces very easy. This makes navigating from tree to tree a breeze.

How we can help:
Buy FSC certified products and avoid purchasing wild-caught pets.

M is for Monarch Butterfly

Region: North America, Oceana,
Southeast Asia

Status: Population Unstable

Facts:
Butterflies begin life as caterpillars, before wrapping themselves in a cocoon and emerging as butterflies. Monarch butterflies migrate as milkweed blooms in different places, and can hibernate for up to nine months during colder seasons. Much like bees, butterflies are pollinators, and are responsible for helping grow food.

How we can help:
Plant butterfly-friendly gardens, and if possible, try growing milkweed plants.

N is for Numbat

Region: Southern and Western Australia

Status: Endangered

Facts:
Numbats are insectivores, meaning they only eat insects. Using a long, sticky tongue, similar to an anteater's, they eat up to 20,000 termites every day. They don't even need to drink water, because of the amount of moisture they get from termites. The stripes on their back help camouflage them from birds of prey.

How we can help:
Donate to programs like Project Numbat and the Perth Zoo to help their captive breeding efforts so more numbats can be reintroduced to the wild.

O is for Orangutan

Region: Rainforests in
Southeast Asian Islands
Status: Critically Endangered

Facts:

Orangutan means "Person of the
Forest." They are known for their
strong, long arms that make swinging
from tree to tree a breeze. An
orangutan mother will care for her
child for up to 8 years; longer than any
other great apes.

How we can help:

Buy products that are FSC certified, and
avoid products containing palm oil. The
trees that palm oil comes from are very
important to orangutans.

P is for Polar Bear

Region: Arctic Circle
Status: Vulnerable

Facts:
Polar bears are the largest species of bears. Their white fur gives them camouflage against the snow, but beneath their fur they have black skin which keeps them warm by absorbing more sunlight. They spend a lot of time walking on ice and are great swimmers. Polar bears are solitary when they're adults, but cubs will stay with their mother for two and a half years.

How we can help:
Reduce your "carbon footprint" by using less electricity, less water and less plastic.

Q is for Quetzal

Region: Tropical Forests of Central America
Status: Vulnerable

Facts:
Quetzals were considered sacred by ancient civilizations in Central America, like the Mayans and Aztecs. Their colorful feathers were often used to show how rich someone was. Their long tailfeathers can take up to three years to grow. Quetzals usually grow to be between 14 and 16 inches, but their tails can get as long as three feet long.

How we can help:
Buy FSC certified products. Trees are important for the birds to hunt and build nests.

R is for Rhinoceros

Region: Africa, India, Southeast Asia
Status: Vulnerable—Critically Endangered

Facts:
Rhinoceros means "nose horn." The horn of a rhino might look like a bone, but it's made from the same material as hair and fingernails. White rhinos are the second largest land mammal, only behind elephants. Despite their massive size, rhinos can run between 30 and 40 miles per hour, much faster than any human!

How we can help:
Contact government representatives to talk about conservation, and send letters to the president of South Africa, expressing your interest.

S is for Sea Turtle

Region: Tropical oceans
Status: Vulnerable—Endangered

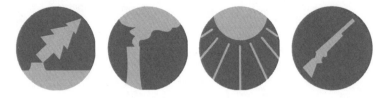

Facts:
Sea turtles are some of the most ancient animals alive today. They have existed in our oceans for more than 100 million years, long before dinosaurs went extinct! They can stay underwater without breathing for up to five hours. Sea turtles lay their eggs at the same beach they first hatched, and some turtles will migrate more than one thousand miles to find their beach.

How we can help:
Use less plastic and be sure to recycle when possible. Plastic bags can resemble food to some turtles, but plastic is definitely not good for them!

T is for Tiger

Region: Forests and Savannas in Southeast Asia

Status: Endangered

Facts:

Tigers are solitary hunters. They are typically nocturnal, meaning they are active at night. Their stripes are used to confuse prey, making it easy to ambush them. Tigers are also the largest cat in the world, with male tigers often growing larger than 600 pounds!

How we can help:

"Adopt" a tiger. Symbolically adopting a tiger can help save them in the wild by providing money to help fund conservation efforts.

U is for Umbrellabird
(Pictured: Long-Wattled Umbrellabird)

Region: Forests in Central
and South America
Status: Vulnerable

Facts:
Umbrella Birds are fairly large birds, with
a wingspan growing up to 18 inches long.
This can make flying in a dense forest very
difficult, so these birds prefer to hop from
branch to branch. Male umbrellabirds fan
out the crest of feathers on top their head
to attract females.

How we can help:
Use FSC certified products. Birds rely on
trees for food, nesting and a place to rest.

V is for Vulture
(Pictured: Egyptian Vulture)

Region: North America, South America, Central Africa, Central Asia

Status: Vulnerable—Critically Endangered

Facts:
Unlike most birds of prey, vultures are social birds. They will take care of their young for as long as eight months, even after the young birds are able to take care of theirselves. Vultures are able to eat meat that most animals can't, which actually helps prevent diseases from spreading!

How we can help:
Eat less processed meats. The crops fed to livestock can often contain chemicals poisonous to vultures.

W is for Wolf

Region: North America, Asia
Status: Vulnerable—Critically Endangered

Facts:
Wolves are famous for their howl. Howls can be used by a lone wolf to alert its pack of its location and they can be used to claim territory. Sometimes wolves will howl just to howl. Wolves are keystone species, meaning they are a necessary part of the food web. For example, less wolves means more deer. More deer means less grass. Less grass means less food for other animals.

How we can help:
Spread awareness! Wolves aren't as dangerous as people think. They will only attack people out of defense.

X is for (Xantus's) Hummingbird

Region: North and South America
Status: Vulnerable—Endangered

Facts:

Just like bees and butterflies, hummingbirds are pollinators, and feed on the nectar from flowers. Their vibrant colors come from the way light reflects off of their feathers. Hummingbirds can flap their wings between 50 and 200 times per second. This incredibly high speed allows them to be the only type of bird with the ability to fly backwards!

How we can help:

Don't use pesticides and plant flowers native to your region.

Y is for Yak

Region: Himalayan region and Tibetan Plateau, Asia

Status: Vulnerable

Facts:
The thick fur possessed by yaks allow them to withstand temperatures as cold as 40 degrees farenheit, below zero. They live in herds of up to several hundered individuals and are typically very docile and friendly towards people. They can use their horns to break through ice and snow to find food.

How we can help:
Consider donating money and raising awareness.

Z is for Zebra

Region: African Plains
Status: Vulnerable

Facts:
Zebras use their stripes as form of defense from predators. Traveling in large herds, the stripes make it difficult for a predator to pick out an individual. The stripes are unique to each Zebra, allowing individuals to be identifiable. Even in their large herds, Zebras tend to stick close-by to members of their family.

How we can help:
Spread awareness about vulnerable and endangered animals!

Want to save the planet?
Make your voice heard!

One person CAN make a difference!

These animals and so many more have been harmed because of the way humans live. The best way to protect them is by telling people about this.

Tell your parents, tell your family, tell your friends.

Contact government representatives! Send them a letter and let them know how you feel about these endangered animals.

Write about them, sing about them, make art about them.

Get the word out!

Even something really small can make a really big difference.